This book is presented to:

_____

This book is dedicated with all my love to my son, Christian. You gave me the greatest joy any parent could have when you asked me to help you find Jesus.

Copyright © 2017 by Sheila Walsh

Published by B&H Publishing Group, Nashville, Tennessee

ISBN: 978-1-4336-8806-5

Dewey Decimal Classification: C232.3
Subject Heading: JESUS CHRIST \ GOSPEL \ SALVATION

Scripture references taken from the HCSB, copyright ©1999, 2000, 2002, 2003 by Holman Bible Publishers.

Printed in Huizhou, Guangdong, China, September 2016.

1 2 3 4 5 6 7 8   21 20 19 18 17

WHERE DO I FIND
JESUS?

SHEILA WALSH

ILLUSTRATED BY SARAH HORNE

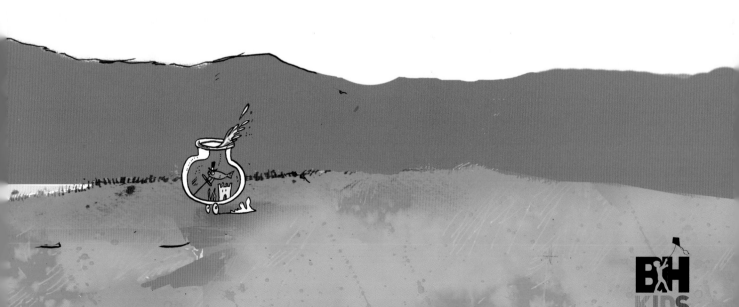

B&H
KIDS

Nashville, Tennessee

"Guess what?" Emma said excitedly to her new neighbor, Abby. "We're going somewhere really awesome tonight. Would you like to come with us?"

"You'll love it," added Emma's brother, Liam.

"It's so cool—you have to go down a GIANT slide to get in!" Emma said.

"Like a water park?" Abby asked.

"Not quite," said Emma and Liam together.

"What do you do at this super cool place?" Abby asked.

"Well . . . we sing," Liam said.

"So it's a concert?" Abby asked.

"Nope," Emma answered. "Not a concert!"

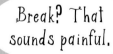
This could be our big break, Wilson!

Break? That sounds painful.

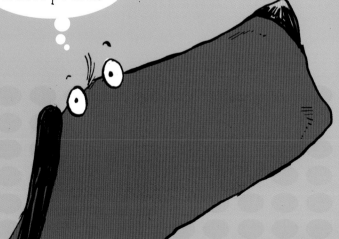

"We make things at this place too," Emma added.

"And we listen to great stories," Liam said. "And we always have snacks!"

"Stories and snacks? Kind of like a bedtime and picnic all rolled into one? I'm in!" Abby said. "Can I bring my best friend, the Bible?"

"YES!" the twins said in unison. "All Bibles on board."

"See you later tonight then," Abby said. "Bye, Emma. Bye, Liam. Bye, Wilson and Charlie!"

When it was time to leave, the twins' mom called up the stairs. "Come on, Emma! Time to go, Liam. Hop in the car! We'll pick up Abby on the way."

"We're coming!" Liam said, taking the stairs two at a time.

"So, where are we going? I can't wait!" said Abby after she joined the twins in the car.

"It's Kids Club at church!" said Emma and Liam together. "You're going to love it. And there's so much to learn. Did you bring your best friend?"

"Ta da!" Abby said, holding her Bible in the air.

"Ta da!" Liam added.

"Ta da!" Emma chimed in. "Then it looks like we're all ready for our special place– Kids Club rocks!"

"Look! Emma cried. "There's the slide. Woo-hoo!"

"Come on, Abby!" Liam cried.

"Whee!"

"Whee!"

"Whee!"

Welcome to our KIDS CLUB

At the end of the slide, Liam introduced Abby to their Kids Club teacher.

"Miss Spencer, this is Abby. She just moved here from America."

"Lovely to meet you, Abby," Miss Spencer said.

"America is all the way across the ocean from Scotland," Liam added. "And it's where hamburgers were born."

"And pies too!" Emma announced.

"Well, that sounds like a delicious place," Miss Spencer said. "We're glad to have you, Abby."

After singing and snacks and lesson time, the kids gathered around Miss Spencer. "So class, what did you learn from tonight's Bible story about Zacchaeus climbing a tree to see Jesus?" she asked.

Several children shouted at once. "I know, I know!"

"Hands in the air, please. Yes, Henry?"

"Sometimes you have to go looking for Jesus!" Henry said.

"Well, that's certainly what Zacchaeus did," Miss Spencer said with a smile. "Emma?"

"And if you look for Him, you'll find Him," Emma replied.

"Did you have a good time, Abby?" Emma asked on the way home from church.

"Did you?" Liam added.

"I did," Abby said. "I liked it a lot."

"You seem a bit quiet," Emma noticed.

"I'm just thinking," Abby said.

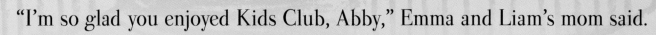

"I'm so glad you enjoyed Kids Club, Abby," Emma and Liam's mom said.

"I loved it!" Abby said.

"But then you got very quiet," Liam said curiously.

"She's thinking, Liam," Emma reminded him.

"Do you think it's too late to look for Jesus tonight?" Abby asked.

"What do you mean?" Emma asked.

"You said in class that if you look for Him, you'll find Him," Abby replied. "You just didn't say where to start."

You're thinking about your next meal, Wilson! It's time to stop thinking. Someone is missing in action. Grab your gear!

"So where DO I find Jesus? I know—He's in your secret cupboard under the stairs!" Abby called as she ran toward the hallway.

"Let's check," Liam said, winking at Emma.

Abby peeked into the cupboard. "No, He's not in there," she said.

"I don't see Him," Emma agreed with a smile.

Come on, Wilson. We have our first lead.

"Is He in the attic? On the porch? Checking the mail? Hmmmm. Where could He be?" Abby wondered. "The tree house!" she suddenly cried. "Of course! Maybe I need to climb a tree to find Jesus, just like Zacchaeus did in the Bible story!"

"All the way up here, and I still can't see Jesus," Abby said sadly. "Maybe I'll never find Him."

"Oh, yes you will," Emma said.

"But where else can I look?" asked Abby.

"You don't have to look anywhere," Emma replied.

"But what do you mean?" Abby asked. "How else do I find Him?"

"Let's go inside for some hot chocolate," Liam said. "We'll tell you all about how to end your search!"

"Here's the not-so-secret secret, Abby. . . . Jesus will come to you!" Liam said. "Just ask Him to live in your heart."

"Yep. I asked Him when I was six," Emma added. "I prayed a little prayer, and now He's with me wherever I go."

"Wow! Really? What did you say?" Abby asked.

"Well, I asked Him to forgive me for any wrong things I'd done."

"I did too. And I told Him that I believe He is God's Son," Liam said.

"Yes! And I thanked Him for loving me," Emma said.

"And I asked Him to help me to live for Him. I also asked if our soccer team could win, but that bit didn't go so well!" Liam added with a smile.

"Would you like to pray a prayer like that, Abby?" the twins' mom asked.

"I would!" Abby said.

"If you want, I could pray and you could repeat after me," Emma suggested.

"I would like that!" Abby said.

Amen! Bow your head, you big lug!

"Dear Jesus,

Thank You that You love me. I want to love You too.

Please forgive me for the bad things I've done.

Thank You that You died and rose again and that I don't have to look for You up a tree. You're right here in my heart now, forever. Amen."

AMEN!

everyone said together.

"Thank you," Abby said.
"Thank you for helping me find Jesus!"

If you confess with your mouth, "Jesus is Lord," and believe in your heart that God raised Him from the dead, you will be saved.
—Romans 10:9

There is no greater joy in life than leading your child into a personal relationship with Jesus. When my son, Christian, was five years old, he asked me to explain to him how he could know Jesus for himself and then to lead him in a simple prayer. It's a day I will never forget! I have watched him grow into the godly young man he is today.

Let me share with you the steps we took based on the truth of God's Word.

We are all sinners. Being a sinner simply means that we want to do things our own way and not God's way. When we disobey our parents or are unkind to a friend, the Bible calls that sin.

For all have sinned and fall short of the glory of God.—Romans 3:23

But, here's the good news! We are all loved by God!

For God loved the world in this way: He gave His One and Only Son, so that everyone who believes in Him will not perish but have eternal life.—John 3:16

God provided a Savior to pay for our sin. God loves us so very much that He sent His own Son to pay the price for our sin.

But God proves His own love for us in that while we were still sinners, Christ died for us!—Romans 5:8

What must I do?

We respond to God's love by believing that Jesus is God's Son and that God raised Him from the dead!

If you confess with your mouth, "Jesus is Lord," and believe in your heart that God raised Him from the dead, you will be saved. One believes with the heart, resulting in righteousness, and one confesses with the mouth, resulting in salvation.—Romans 10:9–10

But to all who did receive Him, He gave them the right to be children of God.—John 1:12

Our family prayer

Dear God, I know that I am a sinner. Thank You for sending Jesus to be my Savior. Thank You, Jesus, for dying on the cross to take the punishment for my sins. I believe that You rose from the dead and are coming back someday. Please forgive me of all my sins, and come into my life and change me. Please teach me how to follow You for the rest of my life. Thank You for saving me and taking me to heaven when I die.

In Jesus' name, Amen.